Holding Space for Joy

A Prayer Companion for Women Struggling with Infertility

MARY BRUNO

OSV
Our Sunday Visitor
Huntington, Indiana

Nihil Obstat
Msgr. Michael Heintz, Ph.D.
Censor Librorum

Imprimatur
✠ Kevin C. Rhoades
Bishop of Fort Wayne-South Bend
April 4, 2024

The *Nihil Obstat* and *Imprimatur* are official declarations that a book is free from doctrinal or moral error. It is not implied that those who have granted the *Nihil Obstat* and *Imprimatur* agree with the contents, opinions, or statements expressed.

29 28 27 26 25 24 1 2 3 4 5 6 7 8 9

Our Sunday Visitor Publishing Division
Our Sunday Visitor, Inc.
200 Noll Plaza
Huntington, IN 46750
www.osv.com
1-800-348-2440

ISBN: 978-1-63966-202-9 (Inventory No. T2896)
1. RELIGION—Christian Living—Personal Growth.
2. RELIGION—Christian Living—Women's Interests.
3. RELIGION—Christianity—Catholic.

LCCN: 2024941528

Cover and interior design: Chelsea Alt
Cover art: AdobeStock

PRINTED IN THE UNITED STATES OF AMERICA

Holding Space for Joy

Contents

INTRODUCTION

You Are Welcome Here

"Suffering is a great grace; through suffering the soul becomes like the Savior; in suffering love becomes crystalized; the greater the suffering, the purer the love."
St. Faustina Kowalska

Whether you're new to the experience of infertility or have been suffering for a while now, whether that infertility is primary or secondary, or you've suffered through miscarriage, I want you to know that you are welcome here. No matter where your heart is — experiencing shame or regret, or feeling worthless, judged, overwhelmed, broken, bitter, confused, tired, disappointed, invisible, angry, bitter, or all of the above — you are not alone. And you are safe here.

You have permission to feel however you feel as you journey through these pages, and I hope you're able to consider this book not so much as a guide but as your companion. This is not a step-by-step process to become fully healed. Only God can do that, with your permission. Rather, this book is intended to present you with some thoughts and questions to take to prayer and consider. I encourage you to honestly search for truth within your heart.

What makes you feel sadness most deeply? What are your fears? What are your deepest desires — even the ones you have never dared to consider or say out loud? What motivates you? What makes you come alive? What is hidden under all the outside noise of your past and distractions of the present? What has really ticked you off? What are the lies that have taken residence within you? Have you been vulnerable with God and your husband? How deeply do you and your spouse communicate?

The journey to discover these things, and maybe even the answers themselves, may be hard. And painful. But I hope that, no matter what, it will be freeing. Healing and discovering yourself fully alive doesn't happen overnight, so the more willingly you enter into this as a marathon — even a lifelong journey — and not a sprint, the more you'll get out of it. Sit with whatever stirs your heart — both the joys and the deep aches — for as long as you need. There is no time limit to your quest, no expectation that you will arrive at any conclusion quickly, or even at all. There is no prescribed routine.

It's just you and Christ, and he isn't going anywhere.

Even if, as I hope, you begin to experience more and more peace and joy as you continue this journey, remember that it's OK to feel all of your emotions — whatever they are. Allowing yourself to know the goodness of the life God has created for you does *not* mean that the source of your suffering isn't very real. It is not forgotten. Joy and pain, sadness and acceptance, can (and often do) coexist.

Infertility has a strange ability to rob us of ourselves as we devote every ounce of our energy and attention to conception. But you are so much more than your good and beautiful desire for a child, and I am hoping to help you remember that, or discover it in the first place. I am so happy that you are here. You are enough, just as you are! As you march forward, always remember the words of the great Pope St. John Paul II: "Do not be afraid."

You are strong, you are worth it, and you've got this.

NINE CONCEPTS

The pages that follow were not written at random. They come from my experience — my life, which became plagued with uncertainty and stirred with a relentless ache to produce new life but was met with a cyclic rejection instead. As time passed and Chris and I still weren't getting pregnant, it got even harder. It felt like everyone around us was having babies — because they were. And they still are.

Almost none of my friends understood what I was going through, and I didn't know of anyone else talking about the struggle of infertility. The lack of awareness was defeating, and there was no roadmap. I was stuck with a deep grief that ebbed and flowed with each passing cycle, and I had no idea what to do with it. Yet in spite of the pain and grief, I can't sincerely say that I wish I had never had this experience.

Although those days were filled with a lot of darkness, they were also days in which God molded me — days when I challenged him and his seemingly cruel plans directly *and* when he drew me deep into the warmth of his heart anyway; days when I toiled to discover my fruitfulness only to realize that it was already there in abundance; and days when my marriage was strengthened because of the many opportunities we took to serve each other and grow in unity.

Infertility brought me the most painful days of my life, but it also forged me into a better person who understands that her worth does not depend on having a child. My worth, like yours, just is and will always be. By the grace of God, I can say that I'm finally on the other side of it, but it's not because I eventually got pregnant — because I never did. It is because I learned how to become open and curious about God's movements. It is because I asked tough questions and was willing to explore and be changed by the answers, because I chose to get back up after falling repeatedly, and because I became more familiar with the goodness within me that cannot be taken away.

I had no idea what I was doing, but the little bit of openness I could muster up was all God desired of me — *my* fiat, *my* yes. I didn't realize it at the time, but that was the invitation he had been waiting for to begin transforming my perception of infertility, and of my worth. And he did. God does not call us to be perfect; he just calls us to avoid staying face-down on the floor when we get tripped up, and never to stop going to him and trying again. He wants you *just as you are* — no matter what that looks like.

I was able to identify some core concepts that I've kept close to my heart and that continue to help me maintain peace. I'm not talking about the kind of peace you receive when you finally get that precious gift you've been asking for, or the kind of peace you feel momentarily here and there. I'm talking about a depth of peace that cannot be stirred or uprooted no matter the outcome of your journey — the kind of peace that "surpasses all understanding" (Phil 4:7), recognizing the weight of the cross you may always carry, but never allowing it to outweigh the true joy of the Resurrection. Because that part is a choice. This is good news because it means that healing is available for you, no matter how your story unfolds.

Suffering through a wide range of emotions, navigating relationships with friends and family who just don't get it, feeling isolated in the Church, getting wrapped up in health issues and treatments, surrendering to God's will, and growing in intimacy in marriage are some important points of conversation that will be addressed in this book. I hope these nine concepts will stir your heart and give you some new things to consider, like they did for me:

1. **Agony:** Be transported to Good Friday and unite your experience to Christ's. Express your raw emotions like Jesus did, without any filters. He understands your pain. Your suffering is not wasted. Learn how to cooperate with it so that it will produce something good.

2. **Isolation:** It is easy to feel alone and invisible when struggling to achieve pregnancy. Letting those who feel safe into the recesses of your heart can be freeing. Know that you and your mental health matter greatly as you navigate friendships and time in the Church. You are needed and valued just as you are.

3. **Curiosity:** The pain of infertility is very real, but it is likely not your only source of grief. Many times, God uses our emptiness to direct us toward other wounds he wants to heal. Learn to befriend your sorrow so it can teach you. Your body isn't the only thing longing to be healed. Your heart also wants to be seen and understood.

4. **Thoughts versus Feelings:** Did you know that there is a pretty big difference between thoughts and feelings, and that how we speak to ourselves can influence how we feel? Becoming aware of these differences can help you distinguish between the lies that you believe and the truth about how God sees you.

5. **Infertility Is a Symptom:** It is not a diagnosis, which means it has an underlying cause (or underlying causes) worth addressing not only to promote fertility, but to promote healing. Sometimes we conflate our body not working the way it should with being broken as a person. Infertility says nothing about who you are. You deserve to be healed whether or not a baby is produced, because you are good.

6. **Pregnancy Not Required:** The pain of infertility is not limited to the absence of a baby. That's just the most obvious hurt. When our will clashes with God's, it causes great friction, which can contribute to the brokenness of our heart. Don't just ask for a baby. Pray that God gives you the grace to trust him.

7. **Discover Yourself Fully Alive:** God is the master creator, and he expresses his goodness in the world through us in a million different ways. Consider your most obvious gifts, desires, and the things you enjoy doing. Look deep inside and think beyond a certain norm to discern how God wants to produce new life through you. There is only one person who can be fruitful like you. You are needed just as you are.

8. **Motherhood, Fruitfulness, and Openness to Life:** Motherhood is not reserved for those who parent little ones. Spiritual motherhood is not a consolation prize. We are all called to make God's love tangible to whomever God puts in our path through the gift of spiritual parenthood. Have you fully tapped into yours? You may have done so more than you realize.

9. **Intimacy between Spouses:** When you're struggling to conceive or maintain a pregnancy, it's easy to forget that a baby should not come first in your marriage. We are called to be united to our spouse before we can raise a child well. Learn how to maintain a rich emotional intimacy by always putting your marriage first.

This book is divided into nine reflections, each focused on one of these nine concepts. In each section, you'll spend some time reflecting on the concept. Then you will pray, using original prayers written by me and a few of my favorite non-profit Catholic infertility organizations. I hope at least one of these organizations will be a good connection for you and continue to offer you solidarity and hope throughout your journey. At the end of each reflection, I have included song suggestions to help you enter in, if music helps you pray. Occasionally, I also recommend a podcast episode based on a specific topic. Finally, each reflection concludes with several journal prompts to help you dive deep into your mind and heart and make this process your own. These are all mere suggestions, though, so if anything doesn't feel right for you, feel free to skip it!

I have organized the concepts by numbers, but they don't have to be discovered in any particular order. The only rule here is to be open and invite God in when you're ready. Let him take it from there. I would also like to encourage you to be open to the idea of finding a good counselor you can trust if you haven't already considered it. Therapists can be very useful in helping us to process the many feelings we are dealing with, regardless of how big or small the problem feels to us.

So let's get started. What matters is not where you are in your journey right now, but where you're going. Our first step will be to lower the temperature a little and acknowledge the truth about how you feel on your darkest days. What are you feeling right now? You may use the following lines if journaling is helpful for you.

1

Agony

"There is no evil to be faced that Christ does not face with us. There is no enemy that Christ has not already conquered. There is no cross to bear that Christ has not already borne for us, and does not now bear with us."
Pope St. John Paul II

How frequently have you imagined that positive test, that newborn in your arms, or the joy on your family members' faces? How much have you wished others understood? Dreams are not in short supply.

The fact that these things seem to live only in our imagination can, at times, be unbearable. We hear that there is life on the other end of suffering, but it often feels out of reach. The part we don't often consider is that, somehow, there is life *within* suffering, within our surrender. Our instinct is to escape the pain at all costs, but I'd like to invite you to lower your guard for a moment and sit with the deepest aches of your heart as we transport ourselves to Good Friday. Express yourself like Jesus did, without any filters.

> He took along Peter and the two sons of Zebedee, and began to feel sorrow and distress. Then he said to them, "My soul is sorrowful even to death. Remain here and keep watch with me." He advanced a little and fell prostrate in prayer, saying, "My Father, if it is possible, let this cup pass from me." (Matthew 26:37–39)

I feel like I have fallen on my face so many times, so these words resonate with me. Jesus' time in the Garden of Gethsemane was shockingly authentic, with no sugarcoating. He was scared. The God of creation cried out for his friends and was left alone and bitterly disappointed. His own Father did not spare him. He suffered extensively and didn't leave out any details about how he was feeling. We shouldn't sell our experiences short, either. We are, after all, made in the image and likeness of a God who grieved and shared his emotions authentically. There may be no better word to describe the discrepancy between the deep desire to carry a child and the daily reality for an infertile woman than *agony*. It is not too strong a word.

The precious time that feels wasted … the guilt of feeling like this is your fault, that your body has failed you … the monthly emotional roller coasters … the loss of life … the many appointments … the financial and emotional expense of treatments … the lack of intimacy during sex … feeling left behind and jealous of others … feeling alone in the Church, unsure of where you belong as one who struggles with infertility (whether primary or secondary) and/or miscarriage … the uncertainty of the future … struggling with connection with and trust in God … struggling with connection with others … and all of this at once? I polled forty-eight women about their most intense struggles on this topic, and these were the most common answers. You are not alone if any of these triggered an emotional reaction. Infertility offers us a very particular brand of suffering.

Many people don't quite understand all the things we are mentally juggling just to survive. While most can recognize that it's hard for a couple not to be able to produce a child they so desperately want, they can't personally feel the ache for a love they might never know. It feels like no one understands, but Someone does. God does. He understands better than anyone else because he felt it too. No one knows those feelings of sorrow, loneliness, despair, and isolation better than Jesus. The agony in the garden shows us that we are seen, down to Jesus' imploring God to let this suffering pass from him.

Still, it often feels like there's a disconnect because Jesus is God. He has the power to take all the pain away. With the snap of a finger, he can make the medication work, help others to understand the pain, cure my disease, fix my husband's health, and give me a healthy implantation. But that's not always what happens. It is completely understandable why so many of us lose trust in God and have a hard time surrendering control. When this happens, turn your gaze to the full context of the passion of Christ, because *Good Friday is the start of something; it is not an end.*

Our God is not a magician who makes pain and longing disappear. He is a lover and a creator with broad, divine shoulders built to carry our crosses on top of his. Love often feels good, but it also hurts a lot. And this is the great lesson of suffering. Love, deep and authentic love, hurts. This is what suffering chisels free from the rock in which it is embedded. As St. Gianna Molla expressed it, "Love and sacrifice are closely linked, like the sun and the light. We cannot love without suffering and we cannot suffer without love." God endured the torture and death of his Son because of love. And the fruit borne from that suffering is the salvation of humanity, which is no small thing. Can you imagine what fruit your suffering will bear?

It is true that transformation and relationship do not come

without great cost. There is no Resurrection without the crushing blows of Good Friday *and* the stillness of waiting through Holy Saturday. There is no love without sacrifice. There is no substitute for the cross, or the waiting. Yet you do not carry your cross or wait in the tomb alone. Jesus could have died and risen on Good Friday, but he didn't. Why? Because there is something sacred and fruitful about waiting and pondering the pains of our hearts.

"My God, my God, why have you forsaken me?" (Mt 27:46). Have these words ever crept around your heart, begging God to answer for what he has allowed? To at least provide some comfort? Hanging on the cross, in addition to his physical and emotional agony, Jesus experienced a spiritual agony too, in complete interior desolation. I know this pain is familiar to many of us. No matter what emotions infertility has ever wrought upon you, you are never alone in your suffering. You are in good company. If Jesus is within you, it is impossible for him not to experience your pain along with you.

When he cries out to God asking why he has been abandoned, Jesus is quoting Psalm 22, which begins with a long lament toward God. If you read the psalm, you can feel the sorrow ripping through the page. But don't stop reading. As the psalm goes on, starting in verse 24, we read:

> You who fear the Lord, give praise! …
> For he has not spurned or disdained
> the misery of this poor wretch,
> Did not turn away from me,
> but heard me when I cried out. …
> Those who seek the Lord will offer praise.
> May your hearts enjoy life forever! (Psalm 22:24–27)

The psalm that begins with so much desolation ends with

praise for God's deliverance.

Then we arrive at Psalm 23: "The Lord is my shepherd, I shall not want" (Ps 23:1, RSV). Those four little words, "I shall not want," could not be more true. When the Lord is our shepherd, there is nothing else we need. That doesn't mean we will have a life free from suffering, but life through it. When God allows infertility and miscarriage, he allows a great amount of suffering. Don't turn your back to it. Cooperate with it, knowing that it will produce something good.

The difference between suffering that bears fruit and suffering that just hurts is our consent to it. Jesus prayed, "My Father, if it is possible, let this cup pass from me." But keep reading. He continued, "Yet, not as I will, but as you will" (Mt 26:39). The result was our salvation. This surrender is what it means to consent to, or cooperate with, the suffering God has allowed. This is a love that will move mountains. If Jesus could accomplish this in the Garden of Gethsemane, he can accomplish it within us today.

Consenting to our suffering doesn't mean that we celebrate it or ask for more. It simply means that we recognize its merit. Your pain is not wasted; rather, you can reverence it for what it is accomplishing. Let's take a moment with that idea. Know that I hold space for your suffering.

PRAY

Dear Jesus, you have given me a heavy cross to carry, and it has become very hard. Sometimes it feels impossible. At times, I feel so angry! I know you've felt strong emotions, too. Sometimes I feel alone and as if there is no hope, and I know these feelings are not unfamiliar to you. I believe that you desire more for my life. Help me to trust you and to choose you no matter what. Sit with me as I wait and suffer in my own agony. Help me to live out Psalm 22 and to be open to your plan for my life today. Help me to trust in your love for me. Give me the kind of peace that surpasses all understanding. I don't know if I am ready and willing to receive all that you have for me, but help me to get there.

LISTEN

- "Hold On to Me" by Lauren Daigle
- "It is Well with My Soul" by Anthem Lights
- "I Got You" by Zach Williams

JOURNAL

What does it mean to you to "hold space" for your pain? To "reverence" it? What does it mean to you to consent to, or cooperate with, suffering?

What are some of the things you have dreamed about happening? If it hurts to think about these things, imagine Jesus sharing these emotions with you as you write. Are you able to grieve the life you wish you had today? Are you able to offer these dreams to God (bearing in mind that this doesn't mean they won't come true)?

Read Matthew 26:36–46. Take notice of how honest Jesus is during his agony in the garden. What do you notice about how Jesus' friends make him feel? Have you made a similar request to the one Jesus makes in verse 39? Verse 40? Even Jesus struggled and expressed his deepest feelings and frustrations. We should do the same.

Can you relate to Jesus' agony in the garden any differently now that you have had a taste from your own life of what he endured?

Have you ever hoped that God would snap his fingers and make a pain go away? Or make something appear? How might that have changed you or your relationship with him or others? Do you think it would have helped, or do you think you might have missed out on something?

2

Isolation

"If you really want to love Jesus, first learn to suffer, because suffering teaches you to love."
St. Gemma Galgani

In one of his lowest moments, Jesus does something that might initially seem surprising. Like many of us, he is inclined to reach out to his closest friends for comfort and solidarity. He expresses something easy to relate to: "When he returned to his disciples he found them asleep. He said to Peter, 'So you could not keep watch with me for one hour? Watch and pray that you may not undergo the test. The spirit is willing, but the flesh is weak'" (Mt 26:40–41). We were made for community, but it's not always easy to find.

How many times have you wondered why a friend or family member could not just sit with you in your pain for a moment? Or why you couldn't be more honest with them? Have you wondered how to navigate friendships when you're in so much pain? Without a doubt, our friends and family members are well-meaning. And some of them, somehow, really get it and are able to enter into our suffering with us and explore the goodness of our unique call to motherhood. If we have just one such companion, our road becomes much smoother to travel, even in all its difficulty. But the reality is that there will be times when we are surrounded by people who are unaware of their effect on the crosses we carry, accentuating our feelings of loneliness.

It can become very painful when conversations are dominated by pregnancy and baby topics; when we aren't asked about what we need, and our gift of spiritual motherhood is overlooked or misunderstood. Often we face a lack of sensitivity in how announcements and invitations are delivered, or in how our "I can't come to that right now" response is received. These things happen every day. You are not alone, weird, selfish, or wrong for being greatly affected by them, but there is something you can do that I believe will ease the tension.

There really is something to be said about community. We were not meant to live with our hearts apart from one another. The Nicene Creed states, "I believe in one, holy, catholic and apostolic Church." Being one doesn't mean that we are all exactly the same, but that we are united in our love for Christ and one another. Christ built us for community. Our differences don't make us less valuable; instead, they should be reverenced as an important part of the Body of Christ. But to give someone else the opportunity to love us, we have to let them in. And that can be really hard.

We can't control how everyone reacts or speaks about topics that are sensitive to us, but we can share the parts of us that are grieving, our hopes and dreams, our victories and setbacks, and our desire to be seen *with those who feel safe*. The pain that you experience due to infertility or miscarriage is a part of you — probably a significant part of you, at least for right now.

Those who love us desire to know that part of us, too.

Our loved ones, and even people we aren't as close to, likely do not want to cause us pain. Although there should certainly be some level of awareness and effort to consider what anyone is going through, women who haven't been infertile or miscarried themselves will have little to no concept of the many things that cause hurt unless we tell them (with love and vulnerability). It is not because they don't care, but because their brains have had no reason to process information this way. Some will make more of an effort to receive you than others, and this may reveal your more authentic relationships. Some may need a little help, brought forth by your vulnerability.

I have spoken to many women about this. For women who are infertile, navigating this difficult life experience with friends and family, and in church, tends to be the hardest part. But I have also had countless women with children ask me for advice about how to handle their infertile loved ones with care. I can tell that they have a deep desire to tend to their hearts, but they simply don't know how. Let in the people you trust. This will help them to understand the words and actions that cause you pain and teach them how to give your heart the love it needs and deserves.

One of my very best friends is a Catholic woman who has had two surprise pregnancies. Although we don't do it perfectly, our friendship has such depth because we are both willing to share deeply about the causes of our grief and fears about the future, and also listen without judgment. We each have the freedom to express how we feel with each other. It is this component of friendship present in her and some other friends with children that frees me to engage more with them, and even in the lives of their children.

This doesn't mean that it wasn't hard when my friend sensitively shared her third pregnancy with me and as she welcomed her new baby home, but the pain did not endure. If she had a baby shower, I have no doubt that she would have understood if I had chosen not to go, and likely would have laid that option out for me — but only because I had already revealed to her how difficult baby showers were for me. She was also able to share her struggles with me, even though many of them were polar opposites of mine. A mutual respect allows me to still share, to some extent, in her pain and joys. The more you share with others, the more you identify the universality of suffering. This has been a shocking result for me as I discover more about sharing my authentic self with those who feel safe.

We also have a genuine appreciation for life outside of motherhood, and the unique gifts and talents with which we each color the world. We believe that the growth of our families is an incredible gift to seek and experience, but it is only one aspect of our very full lives. While we absolutely chat about family stuff, our conversations are incredibly broad and span an array of our interests, weekend plans, struggles, and passions. It is a relationship that supports and encourages the whole person. This is how we build up the people we love.

It takes time to establish this kind of relationship. And sometimes the difficult conversations and invitations come before you have the chance to. Still, please know that it is OK to decline any invitation to a baby shower, birthday party, gender reveal, baptism, or any other gathering that will put unnecessary pressure on a wound you are trying to heal, whether it's coming from a friend or your closest family member. Be respectful, but you do not have to pretend to be excited or display any amount of affection that is not authentic.

This is in no way selfish, but an exercise in honesty and an act of love for yourself and your family because your pain should be honored. Your honesty is good for them and you, and it will hopefully result in a closer relationship. If you believe you need to say no, it is an opportunity to be vulnerable — to tell the truth about how you feel. It may not always be done perfectly, but it gives others a chance to step into your suffering with you.

We can extend our sincere congratulations and warm wishes in the manner that feels most safe and healthy for us. I prefer text messages, but you have permission to choose what is right for you. We can be truly happy for someone else while at the same time feeling grief about our own longings that feel out of reach. Both are acceptable. If we can't hold space for our own pain, it will be difficult for others to do the same.

This may make others uncomfortable, and that can be very hard, but that's also OK. We are all learning how to love, and as we have already determined, that can be a painful process. But *you are worth loving well*, and we are all, hopefully, working to build community. An authentic community is not made up of only joy, or only sorrow. It is made up of a wide range of situations and emotions present within each of its members.

We are made in the image and likeness of God. And God is a communion of persons. He does not exist in isolation. This is something we, as a Church, should understand better than anyone. As Pope St. John Paul II wrote, "Man becomes an image of God not so much in the moment of solitude as in the moment of communion." Our Church should be a place for respite, for being seen, for consenting to our suffering with the support of those around us, and for feeling the depth of our sorrow as Christ did on Calvary.

Some of us have found this in our parish or in a particular priest. Others tolerate the lack of community and awareness of the crosses of others in order to receive the sacraments, where we truly encounter the One who suffers with us best. Some leave and never come back. The Church can become a place of isolation just as much as it can become a place of unity, in part because fostering unity can be very hard work.

For example, every year I learn of more Catholic infertile women who either leave town and go to a different church or skip Mass altogether on the Sunday of Mother's Day. Many priests ask all mothers to stand for a special blessing without also verbally recognizing the gift of spiritual motherhood or those who long for biological motherhood. This emphasizes feelings of isolation and rejection in the infertile and mothers bereaved due to miscarriage. The latter can feel confused as to whether or not they qualify to stand.

Parishes generally do a really good job of creating events devoted to children and families. Finding ways to incorporate those individuals and families who experience life differently has to be more intentional, but at the very least, it helps to make it clear that the church and parish, specifically, suffer with those who cannot conceive or carry a child to term like so many of their counterparts sharing the same pews. The same applies to any person who feels isolated and unseen for any other reason. If we are going to become aware of these needs in our community, we have to start listening and sharing.

When our Church leaders, educators of the Faith, and any other brother or sister in Christ are willing to step into the suffering of the faithful, and when we who suffer are willing to be vulnerable and share that with them, the Church truly grows in her oneness. Fr. Paul West is a priest of the Byzantine Catholic Eparchy of Passaic who is married. He and his wife, Alissa, have two children, but struggled with primary and secondary infertility and loss. He has said that "Infertility, at its core, is truly a matter of the human person, and a struggle that transcends differences in faith, ethnic or cultural boundaries. Infertility wounds those affected physically, emotionally, spiritually, and within their marriages. There are so many couples carrying these wounds, including in the Church. Thankfully, we who bear this burden, and those who support us, are beginning to realize this experience should not be carried in isolation, but in community, and with the help of the clergy and all the People of God. It is during our most vulnerable times that we're most in need of forming community so that together we can come out of our isolation to find strength, support, and God's love for us."

There is power in vulnerability, but vulnerability can also be terrifying. Take baby steps. Get to know yourself and your own grief first, and open up slowly to the people you feel safest with, whether they are friends and family or a priest at your parish. Go at the pace that feels right for you. This is one thing you do have control over! Take some time to appreciate the little things in which you do have a say, even when they may be hard.

I don't think God "chooses" this cross for us, but he does allow it. Our friends and family have their own crosses that are no less significant — just different. Even the way our fellow infertile sisters suffer won't be the same because we are unique and unrepeatable persons shaped by distinct life experiences that, hopefully, draw us into communion with God — and each other. What matters is our individual call to holiness and our willingness to work toward oneness in our love for God and one another. I know it doesn't always feel this way, but you are never alone, and you've got this.

PRAY

Jesus, I feel alone. Sometimes the burden of this cross feels like more than I can handle, and the sense of isolation is like a desert stretching endlessly before me. Yet even though I have felt isolated, abandoned, scared, tired, and helpless while carrying this cross, I know in my heart that you are there. You know the pain I keep hidden in my heart, and the loneliness that sometimes overwhelms me, because you experienced it all on the Cross. Pour your love into my heart and give me courage and strength to carry my cross. Open the hearts and enlighten the minds of those around me, so that they would recognize the weight of my cross and lend their shoulder to hold it up, as Simon of Cyrene helped you on the way to Calvary. Jesus, please give me the grace to pick up this cross daily, to be grateful for the gifts you give me, and to follow you. Amen.

— The Springs in the Desert Team (springsinthedesert.org)

LISTEN

- "Abide with Me" (from *Evensong*) by Keith and Kristyn Getty
- "This Is the Air I Breathe" by Kelly Pease or Hillsong
- "Firm Foundation" by The Belonging Co
- Podcast: *The Springs in the Desert Podcast*, "How to Flourish in Our Brokenness with Liz Kelly" (June 14, 2023) or *The FAbM Base Podcast* with Mary Bruno and Emily Frase, "How to Talk Infertility with Friends and Family" (May 2023)

JOURNAL

Have you opened up to anyone besides your spouse about the difficulties you are experiencing? Name at least two other people whom you'd like to *consider* opening up to when you're ready and how you might start the conversation. You don't have to share every detail with everyone. *You* pick and choose to whom, how much, and when you share. It could be as simple as "Guys, it gets really hard when we spend so much time talking about pregnancy. Sometimes my heart can't take it. Would you mind if we talked about something else?"

Have you declined an invitation to any event that would have been difficult for you? If not, how did going make you feel? How did you feel during the event and afterwards? Did it help your heart or make it worse?

What does it mean to you to understand and value your mental and emotional health? Do you recognize the difference between selfishness and self-care, and see yourself as a gift to be cared for? Do you see self-care as a responsibility to help you love yourself and others well?

What has your experience been with the Church? If there are wounds, write about them here, whether they have to do with infertility or not. If you have been harmed in any way, it's not OK. We, the whole Church, suffer and stand in solidarity with you. We desire your healing! There are people you can trust. If you think you could also benefit from counseling, there are many good options to choose from. If you are looking for a Catholic counselor, visit catholiccounselors.com to connect virtually or catholictherapists.com to find someone nearby.

3

Curiosity

"Anyone who seeks truth seeks God,
whether or not he realizes it."
St. Edith Stein

A couple of years ago, a close friend hurt me deeply. Something I did upset her and instead of talking to me about it, she wrote me two angry letters. I was blindsided. I was then asked not to respond, and that sent me over the edge. I had never been so angry and confused in my entire life and couldn't stop thinking about the situation. There *was* something I should have been focused on, but it wasn't my rage or my confusion. I wasn't dealing with the problem; I just wanted to forget this person ever existed. I was unhinged and this concerned me.

I met with my spiritual director, who challenged me not to enter into replays of the situation or my imagination of what might happen in the future, but to enter into the pain I felt so deeply to try and understand what about it hurt so much. I was invited to, in a way, befriend it and get curious. What wound was it tugging on?

Had I felt these feelings before? What messages were taking root in my heart? As difficult as it would be, I knew this was the right thing to do because I had done it before. Stepping into the pain of infertility had been precisely the thing that triggered my healing when that was my biggest struggle.

So I did. I set aside some alone time and got vulnerable. I asked God to take my hand as I trudged through the anger until I found the place in my heart where I felt the most grief. As Lloyd and Jan Tate explain in their book *In-Home Marriage Preparation*, anger is not a primary emotion, but the result of some hurt, shame, guilt, or frustration that caused it. So it is good to dig until you find the source. For me, it went back years to when someone of significance had made me feel as though my feelings didn't matter and that I didn't have a voice. I felt small and forgotten. This had stuck with me throughout the years, and my friend had unknowingly heaped coal onto those wounds. What she did was wrong, but it was the pain from long ago that made me feel so bad. I needed to invite God to restore my heart by affirming my worth as his child whose voice will always be heard by him. No one can take that away.

What are your main emotions right now? Can you find their roots?

Dear friend, the pain of infertility is real, but it is not an isolated pain. I'm not suggesting that the pain you're experiencing presently is because of something that happened in your past. I am saying that your heart is feeling many emotions that are crying out to be understood. What might your core wound be? Is it possible that something related or unrelated to infertility is tugging on it? What might your pain be bringing up and trying to communicate to you? The only way to learn about this pain is to feel it. This is difficult because the pain can be so strong, but also because it feels unnatural. It is easier to distract ourselves by focusing on what we don't have, on all the time we have lost, and even by piling on treatments. There is nothing wrong with pursuing holistic treatments, but what our *hearts* are longing for is to be heard and understood — to be seen.

There are some of us, on the other hand, who believe that we are called to endure suffering for the sake of suffering itself or based on the inaccurate notion that children are a prerequisite for holiness or openness to life. Treatments and other efforts may be continued to the point of exhaustion not because we are called to it, but out of what we mistakenly perceive to be obedience. When possible we can and should seek to remedy issues that lead to greater unnecessary suffering and to pursue whole health. But suffering over which we have no control can be incredibly fruitful when we cooperate with it and use it to bring us closer to Christ. As St. Teresa of Ávila teaches, "We gain more in one day from the afflictions visited on us by God or our neighbor than from ten years of self-inflicted suffering."

It wasn't until I began to step into my suffering and get real about my feelings that I began to taste freedom. Our initial reaction to grief is typically to reject it in an attempt to leap across Holy Saturday to get to Easter Sunday, but that's not how healing works. Adam Young is a passionate Christian Licensed Clinical Social Worker and Fellow with The Allender Center who hosts a podcast, *The Place We Find Ourselves*, that dives into the effects of trauma on the heart and mind and how to promote healing. He addresses this idea of engaging with our sorrow in many helpful episodes. In "How Healing Happens Part 2," he explains that "it's not that you have to learn to grieve. It's merely that you have to stop refusing to feel … stop closing your eyes to what is true." In Part 1, he describes this as "dipping down into the desert season where death looms … we have to linger in death for a time. How long? Usually a few moments more than we are comfortable with." He continues: "To start with, that might be thirty to sixty seconds. But as we experience the taste of joy and hope that results, we are able to linger longer." It can happen at our own pace, but we cannot experience healing until we dip down into the desert.

As a Creighton Practitioner, I see this in many of my infertility clients. After a few follow-up meetings with each one, and after I go over her chart and make corrections, I put my pen down, look her in the eyes, and ask, "How are you feeling about all of this?" And I watch as her walls slowly tumble down, sometimes as if no one has ever asked her this question before. Maybe she hasn't even given herself permission to consider the answer.

I can't tell you how many times this has happened. It is so interesting to see such a dramatic change when we shift from the science of her body to the condition of her heart as her emotions finally find their way out. We are not just walking body parts. We are whole persons. And in order to heal and taste true joy, we have to befriend and express our pain.

Getting real with our feelings means getting real with God, too. Do not hold anything back from him. Tell him you're angry at him and that you hate his plan, if that is what you feel. Tell him how you've worked so hard to be a good person and that it feels like he doesn't care. Tell him that you're outraged that he has left you behind. Tell him if you feel used. Let him see you. He already knows exactly how you feel, but he wants you to be real with him so a deeper relationship can be forged, and so he can speak truth into the lies and tell you that he hears you.

PRAY

Dear Jesus, I am burdened with many heavy emotions as I grapple with my cross of infertility. Give me the courage to be honest and vulnerable with myself, others, and you about my pain, my anger, and my confusion. I beg of you the grace to persevere in prayer and faithfulness, even when it feels like you have abandoned me to infertility. Give me wisdom to see how my suffering can be fruitful. Bring me through my suffering to a place of healing and peace. I ask you to work with the trust and the openness that I can give you right now — no matter how small that is. Keep me close to you always. Amen.

— Paula Gallagher, founder of Catholic Infertility Resources (catholicinfertilityresources.com)

LISTEN

- "Rescue" by Lauren Daigle
- "Weary Traveler" by Jordan St. Cyr
- "Choices" by Mary Bruno (ViCTRiX — female victor — on YouTube)
- Podcast: Adam Young, *The Place We Find Ourselves*, Episode 13, "Your Wounds and the Path to Healing" and Episode 16, "Why Lament (Surprisingly) Leads to Life and Freedom"

JOURNAL

Take a moment to look deep into your heart. What are you feeling? Write out your raw emotions. No editing — there is no judgment here.

What would you like to say to God?

Have you ever felt like this before? What wound(s) is/are being tugged on?

Read Mark 14:32–72. Take notice of how honest Jesus is during his agony in the garden. What do you notice about how Jesus' friends make him feel? Have you made a similar request to that of Jesus in verse 36? Verse 38? Even Jesus struggled and expressed his deepest feelings and frustrations. We should do the same.

4

Thoughts versus Feelings

"If we turn from self towards God, our understanding and our will become nobler and readier to embrace all that is good: if we never rise above the slough of our own miseries we do ourselves a great disservice."
***St. Teresa of Ávila, in* Interior Castle**

I am worthless. I am broken. I am unworthy. I have done something wrong. I am not as good as [insert pregnant friend's name]. I am inferior. I am insufficient. I am not a good Catholic. The list could go on. Have you ever thought some of these things about yourself? Sometimes we don't even realize how cruelly we speak to ourselves. Sometimes it's not even our own voices that accuse us of such falsehoods, but the voice of the enemy.

Whenever you are able to be honest about how you are feeling, it's important to make some distinctions so you will not confuse your thoughts with feelings.

Lloyd and Jan Tate explain this in their book *In-Home*

Marriage Preparation:

> Feelings are your interior responses to things. They are spontaneous and usually unconscious. Some such responses are anger, joy, sadness, and frustration. Thoughts, on the other hand, are conscious and somewhat judgmental. People often confuse thoughts or opinions with feelings. Whenever you use the expression "I feel that …" you are usually expressing a thought and not a feeling. Feelings can usually be expressed in a single word.

Here is one example: *I feel like God has forgotten me.* Although the word *feel* is used, this is really a thought. *Feel* could even be replaced with *believe.* Isn't that what it comes down to? We often believe that God has forgotten about us. While this is a thought, not a feeling, it does have a profound impact on the way we feel.

For instance: *I feel heartbroken, lonely, useless, forgotten, and sad because I believe God has passed over me.* These are authentic reflections of how one may actually feel as a result of different thoughts. We do not have control over our feelings, but we do control our reactions to and our thoughts that evoke them. A thought can *feel* true, but that doesn't mean it is.

Your feelings are real, but they don't have to be based on facts to affect you.

My friend, it is quite possible that you have thought or believed some very painful things about yourself. But it is not possible for any of those things to be true, because you are far from worthless, broken, or inferior. And this is the truth that God wants to speak directly into your heart. You are remembered, valued, fruitful, and worth dying for. It will take time for these truths to sink in, but understanding the distinction between thoughts and feelings can be a helpful starting point.

The conversations we have with ourselves matter. Over time, our feelings often become a reflection of the thoughts we have believed, whether intentionally or not. So a good step toward finding freedom is to begin seeing these false thoughts for exactly what they are. Lies don't become unraveled in a moment, so be patient with yourself. Be kind to yourself. Take the time to invite God into these falsehoods and believe only what he has to say about *who you are*. That's not as easy as it sounds. It can be very hard to see ourselves as God does — not because of how insignificant we believe we are, but because of how incredibly precious we actually are to him.

When you know this as a fact in your heart of hearts, it will begin to transform your emotions. When you believe it, you will begin to understand that you were never actually forgotten and that God has a plan for your life that is custom made, even though it may not look like what you expected. Because if God really is good, and if he is who he says he is, he can't make mistakes. He can't make something that isn't good. And he made you.

PRAYER

Jesus, I know you love me and that you would never leave me. Yet, in a season of infertility, after a loss, in between appointments, at family gatherings, with my friends, and in so many other situations, I often feel so far from you. I feel angry, jealous, despairing, and sometimes simply numb. Many thoughts often race through my mind, telling me that I am not good enough, that my marriage is not blessed, or that you are punishing me. Jesus, I beg you to speak truth into my heart, root out any lies I am tempted to believe about myself and my marriage, free me from the chains of jealousy and negativity, and bring healing and joy to my spirit. Jesus, when thoughts and feelings that feed doubt and despair wash over me, please flood my whole being with your overwhelming love for me, that I may know the truth of my identity as your precious child and learn to place all my hope in you. Amen.

— The Springs in the Desert Team (springsinthedesert.org)

LISTEN

- "You Say" by Lauren Daigle
- "Look What You've Done" by Tasha Layton
- "Battle Wounds" by Mary Bruno (ViCTRiX — female victor — on YouTube)
- Podcast: *The Springs in the Desert Podcast,* "Taking Captive Every Thought with Sterling Jaquith" (February 23, 2022)

JOURNAL

Be honest: What are some of the thoughts you have believed about yourself, good and bad? Find the lies and cross them out. Circle what is good.

Now, write again about how you have been feeling. How has infertility made you feel? While you may write out parts of a sentence, note that feelings can usually be expressed in one word.

How have other people made you feel? Write the positive and the negative. Feelings are neither good nor bad. They are just reality.

Ask God to show you how he sees you. Write it down. Don't holdback — you're pretty amazing. Continue to be open to how God communicates these answers to you throughout the day. Ask him again tomorrow.

5

Infertility Is a Symptom

"And God saw everything that he had made, and behold, it was very good."
Genesis 1:31 (RSV)

Let's take a break from the hard emotional work for a moment. You've earned it! You now have a lot of new perspectives to consider, both spiritual and emotional. But infertility doesn't just affect us spiritually and emotionally. The inability to conceive a child is also very much a physical reality that often requires physical treatment. And the ways in which we qualify our worth tend to be wrapped up in our expectations of the ways our bodies *should* function.

God designed women to produce children under normal circumstances. So when our bodies don't procreate, that means our bodies aren't functioning properly. What does that say about me as a person? As a woman? As a mother?

Nothing.

It says absolutely nothing about *who you are*. It says that your body is trying to communicate something important to you about your health — and nothing more. Read and repeat: *Infertility is not a diagnosis. It is a symptom of some underlying health situation that needs to be explored and addressed.* It communicates absolutely nothing about who you are as a woman and a person. It doesn't even deny your innate motherhood (I'll explain more in another section).

The way God has designed the body of a woman is intricate, fascinating, and nothing short of genius. Let me be clear: I'm not just describing the beauty of normal fertility. I mean that every woman, regardless of the state of her health, is a work of art because she is a daughter of God. You are a daughter of God. Your body is amazing, and it was built to communicate to you (and to specially trained doctors, if you choose). We are, literally, a bunch of masterpieces walking around.

When our reproductive system isn't functioning properly, it gives us hints. It leaves a trail of breadcrumbs we fertility awareness advocates refer to as *biomarkers*, which are pieces of information women of any reproductive age can be taught to gather and provide to specially trained doctors. Some biomarkers include mucus, variations of bleeding, and lengths of the cycles and pre- and post-ovulatory phases. We need only pay attention to make use of this information. It is valuable whether or not we are trying to achieve a pregnancy. Making use of this information is not part of any artificial reproductive technology, which circumvents the individuality of each woman and treats children as a commodity.

As a Creighton Practitioner, I try to reframe a woman's journey toward pregnancy within the boundaries of a health conversation. There is a time to sit with God in the depths of our pain, and there is a time to sit with a medical professional and focus on improving our health. As my good friend and colleague Lisa says, "I can't promise a pregnancy, nor can any doctor, diet, or speaker. I can teach a woman how to chart her biomarkers and promise to be honest, to provide helpful information, and to direct her to appropriate specialists who will help her to find answers."

Some answers may never be found, but it is helpful to look. It is helpful to look not just because having a baby is your desire and that desire is good, but because God made your body good, being healthy is good, and you deserve to be healthy. While no one can promise a pregnancy or complete healing, Restorative Reproductive Medicine doctors (those who do not prescribe birth control or refer for artificial reproductive technologies), like ones trained in NaProTechnology or FEMM™, have one goal: to restore the woman's health — not to suppress it with contraceptives or bypass the problem with in vitro fertilization (IVF) or intrauterine insemination (IUI). The woman's body is something to be healed rather than manipulated. She deserves to be treated as a whole person.

Although charting can be very good, that doesn't mean it can't bring its own set of very real challenges. It was often hard for me to look at my Creighton chart, especially collectively over time. It felt like a daily reminder of all the things that were "wrong with me." I didn't realize that I had cemented certain expectations about how my chart *should* look, or what I wanted it to produce, inside my heart. When it didn't end up how I wanted, I felt sad, disappointed, and a slipping sense of control. I believed I was less of a woman and inferior to my friends. I cried. I wanted to stop. (And if you feel like you want to stop charting, that's OK! It is good to step back and tend to emotional health whenever needed.)

Thankfully, I have an excellent NaPro doctor who helped me identify this missing piece about my own expectations. I learned to separate the fact that there was something wrong with the way my body was functioning from the lie that there must be something wrong with who I am as a person. I learned that it was constructive to accept the chart for what it said, viewing it in light of my health journey alone. We shouldn't just maintain our health to have a baby, but because being healthy is good and the way God made us is good. I cannot forget that God is in control, regardless of what the chart tells me. Once I began to make that mindset shift, it became less personal. I'm not saying that I was perfect at this task. But dropping infertility into the more appropriate category of *health issue* made it less about me and more about problem-solving — all while maintaining a healthy attention toward my emotions.

We should always have a whole health goal, striving to become healthier mentally, spiritually, emotionally, relationally, and physically. When we are at our healthiest, we are most likely to achieve a pregnancy naturally and maintain it. When pregnancy doesn't occur, we have made improvements to our health and, hopefully, quality of life — and have likely learned a lot about ourselves in the process.

Body literacy can bring up some tough stuff, but it can be very empowering regardless of the circumstances of one's fertility. Marking optimal health as the ultimate goal, rather than pregnancy at all costs, takes some pressure off. Doing so has been much kinder to my emotional, mental, and physical health bottom lines. If the whole health of the individual and the marriage is the goal, this creates the best atmosphere into which to bring a child. And if that child never comes, there will hopefully be space for that pain and longing, but also for acceptance, purpose, and peace.

Just like it is important to take the mask off our anger — a secondary emotion — to uncover the primary emotion that is causing it, it is very good to dig deeper to uncover what is causing infertility. It is healing to see ourselves for who we truly are and identify infertility for what it truly is. It doesn't make us any less lovable or useful than our fertile friends and family members. Our discrepancies don't look the same, but we all have them, and we all hold the same inherent value.

PRAY

Heavenly Father, I hear that you have made my husband's and my bodies good, but it does not always feel that way. I think I am broken and feel lost and tired. I feel like I have been poked and prodded with no end in sight. I have waited and waited, and you ask me to wait more. It seems like my body has failed me. It seems like you have failed me, but I know you have not. I believe that you don't know how to fail me. Please show me the respect, dignity, and intelligence with which you have created my body. Help me to appreciate my body as it is and myself as I am. Show my husband and me which treatments you are calling us to pursue, when it is time to take a break, and if you are ever calling us to stop pursuing treatments. We trust in you and we believe. Help our unbelief.

LISTEN

- "The Artisan (God, Give Me Wonder)" by Brother Isaiah (On YouTube)
- "Oceans (Where Feet May Fail)" by Hillsong UNITED
- "Gratitude" by Brandon Lake

JOURNAL

How do I view infertility?

How is infertility connected to my health? Why is it good to be healthy?

What messages have I allowed the condition of my health to send to my heart? Do I believe that my physical health affects who I am as a person? Has anything my doctor communicated to me helped or hurt?

What does God say about how I am created? Look up Psalm 119:73; Psalm 139:14, 15; Jeremiah 1:5; and Ephesians 2:10.

6

Pregnancy Not Required

"For by doing what God demands of us with total surrender of our innermost being, we cause the divine life to become our own inner life. Entering into ourselves, we find God in our own selves."
St. Edith Stein

At first glance, it seems easy to identify why infertility is so hard: There's no baby. Even after all the doctor visits, timed intercourse, medication, supplements, labs, shots, and diets, cycle day one still makes its unwelcome appearance. Or maybe there is a baby, but pregnancy is not being maintained, and cycle day one rolls around sooner than expected. The pain is unbearable.

So we keep trying and end up putting ourselves on repeat. I made making a baby into my sole goal: religiously following doctors' orders, praying all the novenas, visiting special churches, and finding patron saints of infertility and impossible causes. Sometimes sex became a chore or habit we had to complete on specific days rather than a self-donation of love. I didn't even fully realize that I thought having a baby would satisfy some religious obligation. And each negative test left me in a stressful, anxiety-ridden puddle of tears on the bathroom floor, questioning God's love, my purpose, and my ability to be fruitful. Grieving is good, but there was something more than a baby that was missing.

Praying, following doctors' orders, and timed intercourse can be very good in and of themselves. But I wasn't *just* doing those things out of the goodness of my heart. I put intense and unnecessary pressure on myself because I was focused more on reaching my goal than on loving God, my husband, and myself. My priorities were a bit mixed up.

I didn't realize that I went into marriage believing I was owed a child — and then some. Have you ever held similar beliefs? Although the appearances of the families around us might suggest otherwise, children are not "rights" to exercise at anyone's own will. They are gifts, and gifts cannot be demanded, but must be given and accepted freely. Neither God nor our bodies "owe" us anything, and even as we question God's sovereignty, he brings himself down to our level and chooses to suffer with us through each disappointment. Do we allow him in? Will we recognize that God is moving and provides, even if it's not in the specific way we asked for?

As we go through infertility or miscarriage, we are not just grieving the absence of a baby in our arms. We are grieving the loss of our will, our plans, and our ideas which, for whatever reason, are not lining up with God's at the moment. That hurts so much and often invokes intense anger. Some of us have been convinced that we are not being faithful if we don't stop pushing until we produce or adopt a child. That pain is just as unbearable! To ease the flames of our emotions, we need to try to devote some attention to this discrepancy between our will and

God's. This work is just as important throughout the process as the doctor visits, novenas, and church visits.

I'm not suggesting that God wills us to be infertile, but for whatever reason, he has permitted it. So don't just pray for a baby. Pray for your will to truly be aligned with his, to recognize the gifts he has given you, and to be able to see the goodness around you. Accept his love for you, just as you (and your husband) are. Accept your worth, too.

I've spoken to many women in various places throughout the fertility spectrum. Several who achieved pregnancy after being infertile could identify that even after they got pregnant and had their baby, there was still that sense of struggle because they had never stepped into that pain and dealt with it. They simply tucked it away when they got pregnant. While they were grateful, pregnancy was hard and riddled with fear because they still felt those emotional wounds! Healing is hard work. That pain from wrestling with God and ourselves may fade into the background as it becomes drowned out by bigger and more exciting distractions like a pregnancy, but there is only one way to silence it. The best kept secret to healing from infertility is that pregnancy isn't actually required to find healing and experience true joy. I live this every day.

Remember this: Joy and pain can coexist. I'm not suggesting that being unable to carry your own child won't hurt or that you should try to forget about it. I'm acknowledging that clashing with God's will is different than walking through that tension and finding a way to accept and grow from it, whatever it is. Acceptance is painful, but it also frees us to receive the other desires of our hearts that we may have been too distracted to nourish — other ways in which God hopes to give us joy. He finds value in you for who you are and not for what — or whom — you produce. Now the challenge is for you to find that same value in yourself.

PRAY

Dear God, I have felt so lost. I have desired to have children and you said that was good, but it appears as though we are unable to cocreate one with you, and it hurts deeply. Help me to see children as you see them — as pure gifts, and not something I am owed. Help me to recognize the incredible gifts you have given me. Help me to remember that you are always moving, even when I don't see it. Be with me at each doctor appointment. Help my husband and me to make each act of intercourse a self-donation and an opportunity to grow in unity. Help me to desire your will just as much as I desire a child. See me and love me as I am. Help me to see you and love you as you are. Help me to love my husband as you love him. Help me to love myself as you love me.

LISTEN

- "Still" by Hillary Scott
- "Shepherd My Thoughts" by Brother Isaiah (On YouTube)
- "Thy Will" by Hillary Scott
- "Remember" by Lauren Daigle

JOURNAL

Do you believe that God is moving mountains that you don't see? That he is in control even when it doesn't seem like it?

Do you believe on some level that having children will satisfy a religious obligation?

How did you view having children when you were a young child? How did you view it going into marriage? How do you view it now?

Do you believe that you will only ever be satisfied or fulfilled if you can produce a child?

How have you seen the goodness of God's plan, especially when you couldn't see that it was good at first, as you look back on other areas of your life?

7

Discover Yourself Fully Alive

"We will always find fundamentally the compulsion to become what the soul should be."
St. Edith Stein

When I was younger, I wrote stories, performed magic shows for my family, and recorded audio tapes and videos. I even turned a long email draft on a spiritual topic I was passionate about into a short book (that didn't go anywhere) when I was nineteen years old. My faith was also always very important to me. I was compassionate from a young age and sought to be a part of skits in youth group. I loved to play sports and was pretty good at all of them. I was also very passionate — sometimes a little too passionate. In person, I'd strike you as shy and sweet, but get me on a basketball court and knock me over if you want to see me get real fired up. The two "technicals" I got (meaning I was kicked out of the game) were not my finest moments. It was also on the basketball court in high school that I developed an interest in hip hop music.

When I grew up, I became a physical therapist assistant to satisfy my interest in sports and anatomy and physiology, and my desire to help people. I became a youth minister to make a spiritual impact on teens. As life changed, I continued to get fired up about various topics and injustices that personally affected not only me but also those around me, and I learned to channel that passion into writing, public speaking, videos, rapping, podcasting, and advocacy, and eventually published my first book. These are some of my many gifts. My creativity and unique interpretation and expression of my faith and the world, based on my personal experience and knowledge, are valuable. These are some of the things that make me come alive and that God uses to produce goodness in the world. If you look deep into their roots, you'll see that these gifts and desires have been planted there from the very beginning, and with real purpose. You have some incredible roots, too.

Think about the world from the beginning of time. Can you imagine how many different qualities God has combined in every individual person with all of his creativity? Think of all the important ideas, interesting organizations, useful products, acts of generosity, inspirational thoughts, and gestures of kindness that have been utilized for good. Think of how vastly creativity is used in every single area of life, big and small, none of which would be possible without a person (or persons) saying "yes" to God — whether or not they've realized to Whom they were responding. We tend to forget, or maybe we never truly understood, that a baby is not the only gift. We are the gift, too — as individuals and married couples — and we remain a gift no matter what happens.

There is, and will only ever be, one of you and one of your spouse. God placed certain abilities and desires within your very bones. He planned you, exactly as you are, from the beginning of time with some purpose, and that may or may not include having a child, but it absolutely involves honoring you, your gifts and talents, and the way you were designed to bring about some good in your family, community, and world.

I planned my career around *my* plans for marriage and children before I even met my husband. I knew it was important to discern my vocation and whom God was calling me to marry, but I didn't feel the same need to discern the growth of our family. It was almost as if I had been trained to follow a specific sequence of graduation, job, marriage, children, quit my job to raise children, then have more children — no matter what. This sequence can absolutely be a beautiful calling, but was it truly mine? What I perceived to be this prescribed path for my life caused me to stop exploring the ways in which God was calling me to be creative and fruitful by the time I prepared to graduate college. When infertility eventually crept in, I felt lost and like a failure, and this caused me to question my worth as a wife, woman, mother, and daughter of God.

Fortunately, infertility also challenged me to go back to square one. And I wonder how much less I would have suffered had I been raised to appreciate myself as I was, in all of God's glory, and discern *his* plan versus my plan — or a perceived "Catholic norm" — for my life. I had to wrestle with God and myself to discover when true discernment had stopped (if it had ever started) and adherence to a certain routine shared by those around me had kicked in. Through the exploration of my pain, I discovered so many glorious gifts that were getting dusty on the shelf. There's nothing wrong with getting married and quitting your job to have kids — if that is what God has called you to do. It's just that there is so much more new life God wants to bring into the world besides — or in addition to — that, and sticking to a particular status quo deprives us of our individuality. We are unique and unrepeatable persons, and God's plans for our lives are also unique and unrepeatable.

What if this had been communicated to you as a child? A young adult? At any point in time? If you're Catholic, you've probably been exposed to a valid and needed effort to counter the widely accepted cultural narratives that condone birth control, abortion, and IVF. Unfortunately, the ways in which these causes have been championed have occurred at the expense of a true and robust understanding of fruitfulness. Those who struggle with infertility become collateral damage when spiritual parenthood and the fullness of procreativity and openness to life are not simultaneously championed. That's not your fault, and neither is infertility.

Infertility cannot rob you of your fruitfulness, openness to life, or life fulfillment. You are gifted and talented, and have more purpose than you may have given yourself permission to dream of. You have so much to offer to the world, to the Church! Invite God to show you how. He has been so good to us. Invite him to reveal yourself to you, fully alive.

PRAY

Good and loving God, thank you for the many ways you have created me to bear fruit in this life through the many gifts and talents you have bestowed upon me. Some of these come easily to mind while there may be others I've forgotten or haven't taken the time to discover and explore. While you know that I long to have a child, help me to remember in my infertility journey that by the very way you have designed me, you have already provided ways for me to experience immense joy. Help me to recognize opportunities to produce fruit and to have the courage to seize those opportunities that would glorify you and bless my spouse, my family, and the world. Remind me of those areas in my life where I feel the most in tune with who I am and my desires and strengths. May the spirit of discernment grow within me as I seek to discover your plan for my life and where you may be calling me to direct my life-giving desires. May your will always be done over mine. In Jesus' name I pray. Amen.

— Jen Crowley, director of Sarah's Hope & Abraham's Promise and author of *Praying through Infertility*

LISTEN

- "Goodness of God" by CeCe Winans
- "Reckless Love" by Cory Asbury
- "Pen and the Beast" by ViCTRiX (Mary Bruno) and TwoTen (On YouTube)

JOURNAL

Think back as far as your childhood. What are some things you really enjoyed? What have you always been really good at?

Find five positive things that have come from your experience of infertility. For example, was it the reason you met a new person? Did it cause you to get curious about your health? Did it facilitate deeper conversations with your husband? Did it make you more empathetic? Has it caused you to spend more time in prayer? Take your time. If you can't find anything, look harder!

What are a few things you have learned about yourself since you've been infertile? Are there any desires of your heart that have been benched?

What are the desires of your heart now? How might God be calling you to use them? Consider *nothing* to be too small or too big!

8

Motherhood, Fruitfulness, and Openness to Life

"The woman's soul is fashioned as a shelter in which other souls may unfold."
St. Edith Stein

It is not easy to start discovering ourselves more deeply underneath the many distractions that come with infertility, but it is possible. And this exploration is so rewarding that the journey becomes more and more fulfilling once you take that initial leap.

We started out this journey by diving deep into a discomfort that has become all too familiar. We are so used to pain that we have learned to expect it, allowing it to take over at times. We have forgotten that although we will all experience pain to varying degrees throughout our lifetime, God did not create us to suffer. We are designed for union with him — for joy and purpose! He wants us to be free of the ties that keep us from living our life to the fullest. Sometimes those ties are hard to break. Sometimes we don't realize that those knots can be untied.

I knew I wanted to be a mother from a young age. Most girls do. We joke about future children and play house as if it were ingrained within us. That's because motherhood *is* ingrained within us. If you felt a sting when you read that sentence, you're not alone. But the reason this is such a difficult concept to grasp for those of us who haven't been able to procreate as we hoped is because we have been convinced that having a child is required to express our motherhood, our fruitfulness, and even our openness to life.* One of the biggest lies we face when we struggle with infertility is that we're not a mother.

You are so much more than infertility, which is incapable of depriving you of any of God's plans, motherhood included. If you are a woman, he has planned for you to mother. It is innate. Why else would playing house and caring for little ones be intuitive as a child? Why are we generally so well-equipped to listen, comfort, and serve? Why is it most often women who beautify our homes and physical church structures in service of the church family? It's not that men aren't capable, but God gave male and female gifts that are unique to each sex. We each bring something special, and it happens at any age. Motherhood doesn't wait until we are married to become activated.

Our adopted daughter, Bella, is incredibly sensitive and caring to those who are sad. She is naturally receptive to the needs of others. Thinking of my own childhood, even into high school, I loved to visit and talk with a handicapped lady my dad used to bring to church every week. He brought her to

* To be clear on Church teaching: Having a child (or children) is not a prerequisite for holiness or openness to life. But not using any form of birth control to prevent pregnancy is. Natural Family Planning (NFP) is not a form of birth control, and it is licit. All married couples are called to discern if and when God is calling them to space children with respect to the conditions of responsible parenthood stated in *Humanae Vitae*. Couples with children are also called to be open to life outside of bearing children.

church and joked with her, but I spoke to her heart. My Aunt Bobbie never married, but she retired early to care for her sick father for three years until he passed, and then did the same for her mother. My friend and doctor encouraged and affirmed me before I gave an important talk. The world is starving for the motherhood within all of us, but it is seldom recognized as such. Spiritual motherhood is vastly overlooked and undervalued. To many, it feels like a consolation prize.

But consider that Jesus gave his own mother to all of humanity. From the cross he proclaimed, "Woman, behold, your son." Then he said to the disciple, "Behold, your mother" (Jn 19:26–27). And we are called to resemble Christ and follow the example of his mother, both in raising a child well, and serving the people in our family, community, and church that God has placed there for us, just as we are.

Spiritual parenthood is vital to all humans, regardless of their ability to procreate. To be a mother is to nurture, discipline, comfort, listen, nourish, laugh, serve, create, share, teach — to love well. Having children alone doesn't satisfy our call to be fruitful. Almost anyone can get pregnant, but it takes bravery and many acts of the will to love and raise children, our family, and our neighbors well. *Love* is an action word, and this verb doesn't just make us mothers. It also makes us fruitful.

So what does it mean to be fruitful in our marriage? Let's start to unpack this by taking a look at the Sacrament of Matrimony.

The sacraments of initiation (Baptism, Confirmation, and Eucharist) are aids in someone's personal salvation, but the Sacraments of Holy Orders and Matrimony "are directed towards the salvation of others; if they contribute as well to personal salvation, it is through service to others that they do so" (see *Catechism of the Catholic Church,* 1533–34). Furthermore, each of the seven sacraments makes an invisible reality visible by way of a sign. Baptism uses water to bring about the cleansing it signifies. Like food nourishes the body, Christ in the Eucharist nourishes our soul.

With marriage, the sign is the couple themselves, who exchange vows on their wedding day and are then charged with making Christ's love tangible to each other and the world every single day thereafter. Here's the point: Your marriage is fruitful by the very nature of its being a sacrament.

Every Christian marriage is intended to reflect Jesus' love for the Church. And how did Christ love the Church? He listened, healed, comforted, served, disciplined, created, laughed, rested, prayed, played, educated, died, and rose again. He said "yes" to God with his every breath, and it showed. Everyone felt it. All his actions breathed new life into the world without bringing one physical child into it.

With her fiat, the Blessed Mother didn't just say "yes" to conceiving a child. She agreed to all the joys and deep sorrows of parenting Jesus and ultimately to becoming our spiritual mother. Our fiat will look different, but it can be the same resounding "yes" to the joys and deep sorrows God allows in our lives.

Having children is one of millions of ways in which a "yes" can be manifested, but it is the nature of our "yes" that makes us fruitful, not a child itself. This is not unique to infertile couples, but a call to holiness for every human.

Fruitfulness doesn't have to look one certain way. Married or not, fertile or not, we are his hands and his feet. Childless or blessed with many children, tattooed or pink hair, divorced or single, sick or well, the world needs you. The fact that infertility exists tells us that there are many different ways in which God calls us to be fruitful. The Church needs who you are, in all the richness of *your* motherhood, and she needs the example of your marriage, too. It's literally not the Body of Christ without the diversity that exists among us.

Are you striving to live like Jesus? Then you, my friend, are fruitful!

PRAY

LITANY OF FRUITFULNESS

When I feel forgotten or left behind, **Lord, allow me to see myself as you do.**
When I feel unworthy of your blessings …
When my "fiat" looks so different from others' …
When spiritual motherhood feels like a consolation prize …

When I get used to living in pain and discouragement, **Lord, open my eyes to the opportunities you have for me.**
When I long to use my gifts to bring light and life to others …
When I forget my calling to make Christ's love tangible to my spouse …

When I question my identity and purpose, **Lord, bear fruit in my life.**
When I feel like my body has failed me …
When my arms and womb feel empty …
When I find it hard to feel …
When I struggle to find ways to express my spiritual motherhood …
When prayer appears futile and unanswered …
When ministry opportunities become apparent …

Jesus, open my mind to the fruitfulness you have in store for me.
Jesus, open my eyes to see where there is a need I can fill.

Jesus, open my ears to hear where you're calling me.
Jesus, open my lips to praise the life you've cultivated in me.
Jesus, open my heart to the love you have waiting for me.
Jesus, open my hands to the work that I can do for your glory.

— The Fruitful Hollow Team (thefruitfulhollow.com)

LISTEN

- "To Be Like Christ" by River Valley Worship (Live)
- "Receive Me (I'm Yours)" by Brother Isaiah (On YouTube)
- "By Paths Unknown" by Brother Isaiah (On YouTube)

JOURNAL

Before you read this journal, how did you define fruitfulness? Openness to life? Motherhood? How do you define them now?

How have you lived out your fruitfulness and created new life in ways you may not have realized? How did/does that make you feel?

How is God calling YOU, not someone else, to be open to life now? How is God calling you and your spouse to be fruitful together? It can include something as simple as going to Mass together or demonstrating your commitment to love by holding hands in public or always being kind and respectful. List more than two ways. Write as many as you can find. Take a moment to dream.

9

Intimacy between Spouses

"Love is never something that is ready-made, something merely 'given' to man and woman; it is always at the same time a 'task' which they are set. Love should be seen as something which in a sense never 'is' but is always only 'becoming,' and what it becomes depends upon the contribution of both persons and the depth of their commitment."
Pope St. John Paul II

Infertility has likely stolen attention from countless date nights, daily interactions, and moments of intimacy. You may even feel like this thief has defined your marriage. But it's never too late to restore order. Before there was an infertile couple, there was a man and a woman who fell in love and walked down the aisle to commit to a lifetime together. You had life before infertility or miscarriage, and that life is still there. It can be an incredible treasure to have someone by your side — and not just anyone, but the person you have chosen to become one with and love until death.

Our marriage relationship is the most important one we have on earth, not the one we have with our parents, our friends, or even our children. Our vows are powerful, reflecting the covenantal relationship between God and his people, expressing a commitment that is free, total, faithful, and fruitful. Others should be able to look at us and how we love and see God. If we are living our vows out well, we don't only share God's love with others, but we increase our capacity to be known and deeply loved by our spouse. And that is rewarding! This connection is essential to a meaningful marriage relationship. It is how God designed us. When the painful realities of life, like infertility or miscarriage, creep in, this solid foundation keeps us grounded. It is never too late to form or strengthen this foundation.

The foundation of a family isn't started with the firstborn child, but on the couple's wedding day. Husband and wife form a family; isn't that beautiful? From that day on, our mission is to love each other as Christ loves the Church — a love that is incredibly fruitful. Sometimes that love comes in the form of a child, but it always comes in the form of loving the people God calls us to love, in whatever way he asks of us. Either way, it is the marriage itself that establishes the fertile soil, and not the physical state of fertility.

So, how is your marriage relationship?

For some, this is easy to answer; for others, not so much. That's OK. Many of us never received a model of a good marriage, and marriage prep often lacks serious quality control. Even with good lessons and models, putting it all into practice with two unique people and two unique families of origin is not easy. Chris and I were fortunate to connect with the creators of a successful marriage preparation program, Lloyd and Jan Tate, who created the "In-Home Marriage Prep" program. They trained Chris and me to become mentors, and this has transformed our understanding of the sacrament.

One of the most profound insights we've found through our work with this program for growing intimacy in the marriage relationship is that it all starts with communication. It's not sex, prayer, or conflict that sets the pulse of the relationship, but the *depth* of communication. Prayer is vital, of course, but even that requires vulnerability. Most of us talk to people every day at various depths, but we mainly stick to the three most superficial levels: small talk, sharing of facts, and sharing of opinions. The two deepest levels of communication, however, are sharing feelings, then needs.

With each level, we reveal a little more about ourselves and become more selective about the people to whom we reveal ourselves. It gets harder to divulge the deeper we go because this increases our risk of getting hurt, but it also increases our ability to become deeply known and deeply loved. We have to be able to trust each other to communicate deeply. Many marriages rarely get past levels 1 to 3. To experience the depth of love and wholeness that God desires for us, we should be communicating with our spouse regularly at levels 4 and 5 — feelings and needs — which brings us back to vulnerability. There is no other way to grow in intimacy.

Our feelings and needs reveal us at our deepest levels, and sharing these things with each other is what we signed up for when we exchanged vows. But being vulnerable is only half the battle. We should also make it our goal to understand our spouse's feelings and meet his needs. The more we each reveal about ourselves, the more united we can become, and that unity is very important because it is one of the *two* primary purposes of intercourse. The other one is procreation, but when procreation gets (often unintentionally) elevated over unity, sex becomes stale, and the relationship loses some degree of warmth. The couple has, basically, begun to lose sight of one another.

Fertility issues are draining and affect us deeply. It is not unusual in these situations for sex to become a chore or a box to check on specific days in the woman's cycle, rather than an act of love that unites and brings new life into the world in some way. Because intercourse with our spouse tends to uncover the deeper parts of ourselves, whether what's underneath is healthy or wounded, this is often where a lack of intimacy in other areas of the relationship will be felt. How could it not, if we are really becoming one?

So, how we navigate our victories and crosses with each other, whether related to infertility or not, matters. Our big and small daily interactions matter because sex begins outside of the bedroom with how we love each other. It is not a separate or distinct part of marriage, but an extension of the whole relationship — "an expression of our unity and intimacy" according to Lloyd and Jan Tate.

What do you express to your spouse during sex?

Whether we have children or not, and even whether we are trying to conceive or not, the purpose of sex for all married couples remains the same: to unite our whole selves in such a way that new life will be produced. I find great comfort in knowing that I am just like every other married couple in this way. We should all be loving each other in such a way that sex becomes, at some point, a natural extension (in two physically and emotionally healthy married adults) of the interactions throughout each day and the depth of love we have chosen to pursue over time.

Yes, target fertile days. But also make a sincere effort to come together outside of the fertile window, too. If either of you is physically, mentally, or emotionally drained during your fertile window, find another way to love each other that night. Forcing or tolerating sex just to make a baby, fulfill a perceived duty, or satisfy a spouse alone undermines the integrity of a sexual act that is meant to be fully enjoyed by both the man and the woman. Removing the unitive purpose deprives a potential child of being created through a sacred act of love and self-donation. Putting our spouse and our marriage first doesn't come without great sacrifice, but it's sacrifice that results in deep satisfaction.†

So how do we grow a deep emotional and spiritual intimacy? Here are a few ideas:

- Don't just talk about how work, managing the house, or a doctor appointment went in a day, but talk about how different events and people made you feel.
- Communicate your needs in a respectful way. Don't assume the other person knows.
- Ask questions, and make sure some go deeper and are open-ended.
- Lovingly reveal how your spouse may have hurt you.
- Share your deepest fears and concerns. Just because it is hard to hear or say doesn't mean it's not loving to share it.
- Listen to your spouse's heart. Feel sad together. Don't forget that the men in our life grieve and process things very differently than we do, but that infertility and miscarriage affect them deeply, too.
- Speak to each other with respect.
- Serve each other daily.
- Apologize.

† If sex is physically painful, it will be physically and mentally harmful to push through it. Sex should never be painful or persist in discomfort. Seek healing through a trusted counselor and/or pelvic floor physical therapy. Learn more at fabmbase.org > resources > external resources > sexual health.

- Learn each other's love languages and use them frequently.
- Share your passions!
- Be silly together.
- Share your struggles with Church teaching, but also refer to the *Catechism* and a trusted priest or friend.
- Pray together in ways that work for each of you. Some people appreciate more contemplative prayer; some are more comfortable with prayers that have already been written for them; some say what's on their heart; and some pray by doing things with love. All are good options.
- Consider going to therapy — individual and/or marriage counseling. This is not only for people with huge traumas or marriages on the brink of divorce. A good counselor can be a vehicle for true personal and relational healing.

It's easy to skip over this part because it seems so simple and intuitive, but it is not always easy to communicate well. This part of the relationship has to be intentional, and it has to be a decision we make out of love every day. It is the only way to grow in intimacy. It is the only way to remember, and continue to get to know, the whole person of our spouse. Infertility wreaks enough havoc. It doesn't have to rob us of our fruitfulness or our relationship. Instead, it can be one source of many that brings us closer together.

PRAY

Come, Holy Spirit. God, thank you so much for the gift of my spouse and the gift of the sacrament you have called us to. Thank you for the gift of our joys and trials, and the graces you give us by way of this holy sacrament. Help us to remember to ask for more graces from your inexhaustible font of love and mercy. Help us to seek you through our trials so that they become doorways to intimacy. Make us good discerners. Help us to continue to learn about each other and never stop our pursuit of intimacy. Take down any walls either of us have put up to protect ourselves from going deeper. Help us to be authentic with ourselves and one another. We invite you to remain the third person of our marriage.

LISTEN

- Your wedding song
- "First Love" by Kari Jobe
- "Love Like This" by The Belonging Co
- Podcast: *Interior Integration for Catholics* with Dr. Peter T. Malinoski, episode 58, "The Catholic Marriage Bed"

JOURNAL

Briefly write out your love story. Describe how you felt when you first met your husband. What made you fall in love with him? When did you know you wanted to marry him? What are your favorite things about him today? Remember the feelings this exercise stirs up, and the reasons you chose each other in the first place, and try to think about these things often.

What is the deepest level at which you believe you and your husband communicate regularly? The levels (according to the "In-Home Marriage Prep" program) are 1) small talk, 2) sharing of facts, 3) sharing of opinions, 4) sharing feelings, and 5) sharing needs. Do you ever reach levels 4 or 5? If so, how often? Does it feel uncomfortable to think about sharing your deepest feelings and needs? If so, why?

Consider how uniting through intercourse has been with your spouse both before you were trying to achieve pregnancy and currently. Has there been a shift? Do both of you enjoy being intimate with one another each time? Journal about how you and your spouse can maintain sex as both unitive and procreative. Remember that "procreative" refers to how your union brings about new life in some way.

Has sex brought up any issues between the two of you, whether they have been shared yet or not? Whether it is good or in need of healing, what has sex revealed to you about yourself? Your spouse? If you can't think of anything, take it to prayer and think about it some more.

List at least three new ways in which you'd like to grow in intimacy with your spouse. Consider physical touch (outside of sex) and spiritual, intellectual, emotional, communicative, and recreational ways you can connect. Does anything else come to mind?

CONCLUSION

You Are Seen

"The glory of God is a human being fully alive!"
Saint Irenaeus

St. Edith Stein said: "The world doesn't need what women have. It needs what women are." This quote gives me so much hope because its focus is not on my physical body, or on what or whom I can produce, but on who I am. Unlike the focus in our culture, and even sometimes in our Church, what the world needs is, essentially, how I love. When all the things I cannot control have become so evident, who I become is still my choice. That is something I will always have control over. And the more I choose to become the woman God made me to be, the more I will recognize myself as his daughter.

But even as we recognize our immeasurable value, infertility still just hurts. Maybe the words, the prayers, the songs, the journaling, the solidarity have been great, but they can't satisfy the longing in your heart to grow a new life and hold him or her in your arms — to see your features reflected in another human. My friend, I know that it doesn't satisfy that longing, and it's not supposed to. No book, speaker, doctor, or minister is going to take away the pain of infertility. But with your "yes," infertility can become the suffering that drives your search for healing and deeper conversion — unity with God and your spouse, improved health, the search for wholeness, purpose, and the truth about yourself.

We can help each other with new language to describe the aches within our hearts and the desires to which we want to give new life. We can help each other get to the root of the pain. We can remind each other that we are not defects of God's design and that he values us just as much as every other human. Our purpose and fulfillment as a woman is just as important. *We are just as capable of producing new life.* To promote community, we can encourage each other to be vulnerable and honest with those around us about the pain and hope we experience.

We can help each other feel seen. Regardless of fertility status, every human has a wound. Every human has aches. You might always feel the ache of infertility, or you might not. I am now permanently infertile, so I know I will, but that doesn't mean I haven't known healing. I know joy and peace, and I have purpose. No matter how deep you feel like your ache runs, there is an ache that runs even deeper. And that's the God-shaped hole that resides in all our hearts. God alone can fill every void and satisfy every longing, because you're not only longing for a child. *You* are longing to be seen.

And God sees you. He sees your pain and suffers with you. He sees your joy and rejoices with you. He sees every part of you and chooses you. He doesn't call you "infertile one" or "broken" or "different." He calls you by your name! Sometimes we have to use them for descriptive purposes, but I don't like the terms *fertile* or *infertile* because there is nothing infertile about me — or you!

During prayer, a friend of mine heard God speak to her heart: "Who told you you were infertile?" I got chills when she shared this with me. You are so much more than your good and beautiful desire to have a child. God wants who you are, just as you are. And we, the world, want who you are, too. As I mentioned before, no book or journal can take away your pain, but I do hope this one has helped you to feel a little more seen and celebrated.

I'm praying for and walking with you, sister. May you discover yourself fully alive and always hold space for joy!

About the Author

Mary Bruno is the author of *Twelve Stripes Deep: How Infertility & Other Suffering Delivered My Greatest Joys* and *Missing Pieces: Female Perspectives on Sex for Catholic Women*, co-founder and executive director of the non-profit FAbM Base (fabmbase.org), speaker, and Creighton Practitioner. She is from New Orleans, Louisiana, where she met and married her husband of eleven years. They adopted their daughter in 2016 and have been a marriage prep mentor couple since 2018. A late endometriosis diagnosis inspired Mary to improve fertility awareness and women's health education through speaking, writing, and social media outreach. Now permanently infertile, her many years of suffering forged deeper conversion and curiosity about understanding her worth and how God calls all women to be fruitful. You can find her unique approach to infertility and sexual health conversations on social media @WhiteLotusBlooming and connect for personal coaching at marygbruno.com.

